Do Gerbils Go To Heaven?

David Henry Wilson was born in London in 1937, and educated at Dulwich College and Pembroke College, Cambridge. He now lectures at the universities of Bristol and Konstanz, West Germany, where he founded the student theatre. His plays have been widely performed in England, America, Germany and Scandinavia, and his children's books – especially the Jeremy James series – have been translated into several languages. His novel *The Coachman Rat* has been acclaimed in England, America and Germany. He is married, with three grown-up children, and lives in Taunton, Somerset.

Do Gerbils Go To Heaven?

David Henry Wilson

ILLUSTRATED BY

Axel Scheffler

MACMILLAN
CHILDREN'S BOOKS

First published 1996 by Macmillan Children's Books

a division of Macmillan Publishers Limited
25 Eccleston Place, London SW1W 9NF
and Basingstoke

Associated companies throughout the world

ISBN 0 333 66203 2

Text copyright © David Henry Wilson 1996
Illustrations copyright © Axel Scheffler 1996

The right of David Henry Wilson to be identified as the
author of this work has been asserted by him in accordance
with the Copyright, Designs and Patents Act 1988.

1 3 5 7 9 8 6 4 2

A CIP catalogue record for this book is available from
the British Library

Phototypeset by Intype, London
Printed by Mackays of Chatham PLC, Kent

In memory of Herta Ryder
who was special

Contents

CHAPTER ONE

Hospital Fish

"Ouch!" said Jeremy James. And then, as nobody took a blind bit of notice: "Owowow!"

It wasn't surprising that nobody took any notice, as Jeremy James at this moment was lying all alone on the lawn with his tricycle on top of him. If Mummy or Daddy had been in the garden, they would have seen the crash and heard the result, but Mummy was in the twins' room removing Jennifer's nappy, and Daddy was in London looking for the place where he was supposed to meet somebody. Jeremy James could have said a hundred ows and ouches (in fact he did say quite a few more), and still nobody would have heard.

The accident had happened when Jeremy James had been chasing a bank robber, for whom there was a reward of ten thousand pounds and a never-ending supply of liquorice allsorts. He had been pedalling at top speed along the garden path. Then, as he had hurtled round a bend with a screech of voice-brakes, he and the tricycle had left the path and come crashing down on the lawn.

"*Owowowowouchouchouch*!" cried Jeremy James once more, but apart from a hopping grasshopper and a wiggling worm, there was no sign of life anywhere. Even the bank robber had escaped.

Jeremy James worm-wiggled his way out from under the tricycle, and then he sat up to find out how much pain he was in. Fortunately, the grass had broken his fall, and the hard bits of the tricycle had landed over the soft bits of his leg. The only thing that really hurt was his left wrist. He had put his hand out as the tricycle had keeled over, and so his wrist had taken all his weight as he fell.

It really was painful. It got more painful as he looked at it. It was a sharp pain, and its sharpness seemed to jump from his wrist straight up into his eyes, because suddenly there were tears dripping down his cheeks. And it didn't stop at his eyes. A fraction of a second later, it had got into his voice as well. Now the sound that came out was less of an ow and an ouch than a wah and a woo, and Jeremy James scrambled to his feet, held his left wrist in his right hand, and wah-wooed his way back to the house.

"What's the matter?" asked Mummy, as Jeremy James came wah-wooing into the twins' room.

Jeremy James showed her what was the matter, and a very painful matter it was too. His wrist was red and it had started to get bigger.

"Does this hurt?" asked Mummy, poking it with her finger.

"Owowow!" said Jeremy James.

"It's a bit swollen," said Mummy. "You might have broken it."

Jeremy James had a quick look. He'd seen broken pencils and broken toys and all the things that Daddy broke when he was doing repairs, and they always finished up in pieces. His wrist wasn't in pieces. His wrist was still on the end of his arm, next to his hand.

"It's ... not ... broken, Mummy," he said between wahs and woos. "It's ... damaged."

Nevertheless, Mummy decided that Jeremy James and his wrist should be seen by a doctor.

"Jem Jem cwy," said Jennifer, as Mummy finished changing her nappy.

"So would you cry if you'd hurt your wrist," said Mummy.

"Jem Jem hurty wist!" laughed Jennifer.

"And Jeffer dirty bottom!" said Mummy.

"Wiffer clean bottom," said Christopher, who was sitting in his cot playing with his big toe.

And when everyone had finished commenting on the crying, the hurt wrists and the dirty bottoms, Mummy went downstairs carrying Christopher and Jennifer, while Jeremy James went downstairs carrying his left wrist.

Fortunately, Daddy had gone to London by train, because that made it easier for him to find his way, and so the car was ready and waiting outside. Mummy strapped Jeremy James, Christopher and Jennifer into the back, and away they all went to hospital.

The entrance to the hospital was a big glass door, which suddenly split into two in order to let them in. And then, when they had gone inside, it closed itself up into one again. If Jeremy James had not been busy holding his wrist, he would certainly have gone back to make the door re-self-open and re-self-close. But instead he followed Mummy across a large room to a sort of counter where a grey-haired lady sat writing in a book.

"Hello," said the grey-haired lady, looking up.

"Hello," said Mummy, looking down.

"Lift Jeffer!" cried Jennifer.

Mummy lifted Christopher and Jennifer on to the

counter, and Jennifer smiled at the grey-haired lady while Christopher looked at her and didn't smile.

"Oh, what lovely children!" said the grey-haired lady.

"Luvvy," confirmed Jennifer, smiling even more sweetly.

"This is the patient," said Mummy, and the lady looked down at Jeremy James.

"Oh dear," she said. "And what have you done, young man?"

The young man told her that he'd damaged his wrist and it was very painful. And Jennifer told the lady that Jem Jem had hurty wist and Jeffer had had dirty bottom.

The lady took down some details (though not about Jennifer's dirty bottom) and then asked Mummy to wait while she told the doctor. There were quite a lot of chairs round the walls of the large room, but only a few people were sitting there.

Mummy, Jeremy James and the twins sat near an elderly man with bristles and an elderly woman with a stick.

"'Urt yerself, 'ave yer?" asked the man.

"Yes," said Jeremy James. "I've damaged my wrist. I fell off my tricycle."

The man said that his wife had damaged her ankle, without falling off her tricycle. She'd fallen downstairs instead. And now she was waiting for the X-ray result.

"What's an eggs-ray?" asked Jeremy James.

"It's a pickcher of yer bone, ter see if it's broke or not," said the man.

Jeremy James looked at the lady's ankle, and saw that it was all in one piece between her leg and her foot.

"It's not broken," he said.

"That's a relief," said the man. "We c'n go 'ome now, Doris."

The elderly lady smiled for the first time.

"I fink 'e's lookin' at the wrong ankle," she said.

Just then a young, rosy-cheeked lady in a blue uniform came across the room.

"Jeremy?" she asked.

"Jeremy James," said Jeremy James.

"Ah!" she said. "Well, Jeremy James, would you like to come with me?"

"Shall I come too?" asked Mummy.

"It looks as if you've got your hands full already," said the nurse. "I'll take him."

And so – still holding his left wrist in his right hand – Jeremy James walked alongside the nurse.

"How did you hurt yourself?" she asked.

"I was chasing a bank robber," said Jeremy James.

"Oh?" said the nurse. "I hope you caught him."

"No," said Jeremy James. "Because I fell off my tricycle."

The doctor had a white coat, thinning red hair, twinkling blue eyes, and a painful way of waggling Jeremy James's left wrist.

"Does that hurt?" he asked.

"Owowow!" said Jeremy James.

"That sounds like yes," said the doctor. "Let's get it X-rayed, eh? You know what an X-ray is, Jeremy James?"

"Yes," said Jeremy James. "It's a picture of your bone to see if it's broken."

"Clever lad!" said the doctor.

"But it isn't broken," said Jeremy James.

"How do you know?" asked the doctor.

"Because if it was broken," said Jeremy James, "my hand would have fallen off."

The nurse took Jeremy James along a corridor, round a bend, along another corridor, through some glass doors, and down a passage. He saw lots of doors and windows, a wheelchair here, a trolley there, a man on crutches, a woman in a dressing-gown, a man in a white coat, and a very interesting fish-tank with fish and bubbles and bits of green. He would have liked to have a closer look at the fish-tank, but the nurse was hurrying along, and so he hurried along with her.

When they came to the X-ray department, the nurse handed him over to another young lady with glasses and a tightly tied pigtail.

"Yes, I'll look after him," said the pigtailed lady. "Just wait here, Jeremy James, and I'll come for you as soon as I'm ready."

She disappeared into a dark room, and closed the

door. Jeremy James sat on a red chair, and looked around. There were three other chairs, all empty, a little table with some old magazines, and nothing and nobody else.

Jeremy James's thoughts turned to the fish-tank. Now *that* would be interesting. He wouldn't mind waiting for the pigtailed lady at the fish-tank, because then he'd have something to look at. Fish, for instance. And after all, the pigtailed lady had said she'd come for him when she was ready, and it wouldn't make any difference to her if he was sitting in a red chair or standing beside a fish-tank.

Jeremy James gently slid off the chair, taking care not to bump his damaged wrist, and set off up the passage towards the glass doors. On the other side of these were several corridors that went in different directions, but he was pretty sure that the fish-tank was along *that* corridor, and so that was the corridor he took.

The fish-tank wasn't along that corridor. There were doors, windows, another trolley, a long-haired young man who said hello, a bald-headed man who didn't say hello, and a fat lady with a broom who didn't see him.

Maybe the fish-tank was along *this* corridor . . . No, there didn't seem to be anything at all along this corridor . . . In fact this corridor just led to another corridor, but at least there was someone in the other corridor – a black lady pushing a trolley of tea and sandwiches.

"Excuse me," said Jeremy James.

"Hello, dear," said the black lady.

"Can you tell me the way to the fish-tank?"

"Fish-tank?" exclaimed the lady. "You won't find no fish-tank here, dear, this is a hospital."

"There *is* a fish-tank, because I've seen it!" said Jeremy James.

"Then it must be in the kitchen," said the lady. "Just go down the corridor, and turn to the right. That way . . ."

She pointed.

"Thank you!" said Jeremy James.

"Here," she said. "Have a piece o' fruit cake."

Jeremy James thanked her even more, and with fruit cake in hand and mouth set off down the corridor. The black lady watched him go, shook her head, and pushed her trolley through a swing door, muttering, "Fish-tank. I never seen no fish-tank. I thought they got their fish from the fishmonger."

The kitchen was full of pots and pans and big ovens and steam and people in white coats and hats.

"Hullo, there!" said a red-faced, black-moustached, bushy-browed man. "Enjoying our fruit cake?"

"Yes, thank you," said Jeremy James.

"Then have another piece."

Jeremy James didn't say no.

"Visiting somebody, are you?"

"No," said Jeremy James. "I've hurt my wrist."

"Didn't think our fruit cake was that heavy," said the man.

He and another white-hatted man laughed.

"Where's your mother, sonny?"

"She's over there," said Jeremy James, vaguely waving his fruit-cake-holding hand. "With Christopher and Jennifer."

"Ah," said the man.

"Can you tell me where the fish-tank is?" asked Jeremy James.

"What fish-tank?" asked the man.

"The one with fish in it," said Jeremy James.

"Anybody seen a fish-tank?" the man called out.

"Try the fishiotherapy department," said the other white-hatted man, and everybody laughed.

Meanwhile, the young lady with glasses and the tight pigtail had said goodbye to a fair-haired man with an ear-ring and a limp, and was gazing at the empty red chair on which Jeremy James had been but was no longer sitting.

"Oh!" she said.

She looked up the corridor, looked down the corridor, looked right, looked left, said "Oh!" again, called out "Jeremy James!" a few times, and then stood still and thought. Perhaps the boy had gone back to his mother in the waiting-room.

She hurried to the waiting-room, but there was no sign of Jeremy James. A lady was sitting there with two toddlers, and the grey-haired receptionist confirmed that that was Jeremy James's mother.

11

The receptionist and the pigtailed lady whispered to each other:

"Should I tell her?"

"Well, I don't know. Don't want to worry her."

"Supposing we can't find him?"

"He must be somewhere."

"Supposing he's been kidnapped?"

Whisper, whisper.

In the end they decided that the pigtailed lady should organize a search, and the receptionist should tell Jeremy James's mother.

"Anything wrong?" asked Mummy, as the grey-haired lady came frowningly towards her.

"We seem," said the grey-haired lady, "to have mislaid your son."

"Mislaid?" echoed Mummy.

"Well . . ." said the grey-haired lady, "one moment he was sitting quietly outside the X-Ray room, and the next moment . . . well . . . he wasn't."

"I expect he's wandered off somewhere," said Mummy.

"We've organized a search," said the lady. "He can't have gone far."

Before long, there were nurses, porters, and even patients going round asking if anyone had seen a little boy wearing a smart red pullover and holding his left wrist in his right hand. Quite a lot of people had seen him: a young man with long hair remembered saying hello to him, a black lady with a trolley had given him some fruit cake, the cooks in the kitchen had given him more fruit cake, and a doctor and two nurses and three visitors and four patients had all seen him at different times and in different places. But where was he now? Nobody knew. The only clue was that he'd been asking for the fish-tank.

The pigtailed lady knew all about the fish-tank, and her hopes rose, but when she got there, her hopes sank. The fish were there, but Jeremy James wasn't.

Then an old lady said she'd seen a little boy walking hand in hand with a man in overalls, and they'd left the hospital. She couldn't remember what the little boy was wearing, but it *might* have been a red pullover.

At this news the pigtailed lady burst into tears, and a doctor said it was time to send for the police, and the grey-haired receptionist told Mummy not to worry, and messages were sent to every ward and every department, and several porters went out to search the car-parks and the gardens.

Meanwhile, Jeremy James had wandered through an open double-door and found himself in a large, bright room. There were colourful pictures on the walls, two tables with toy telephones, a rocking-horse with a little girl on it, a tank with a little boy in it, a doll's house, a slide, and more toys and more children.

"Hello," said a boy the same age and size as Jeremy James.

"Hello," said Jeremy James.

"Would you like to play telephones with me?"

"Yes, please," said Jeremy James. "Only I've got

to have an egg-ray when the pigtailed lady comes."

The other boy, whose name was Simon, said he'd just had a sandwich and some fruit cake, and he wouldn't want an egg-ray on top of all that.

With all the wandering and fish-hunting and fruit cake-eating and wrist-damage, Jeremy James was beginning to feel quite warm, and so very carefully, so as not to hurt his wrist, he took off his red pullover, and put it on the floor under a chair. Then he and Simon sat at the tables with the toy telephones.

At that moment a round-faced smiley nurse poked her head round a door and called out: "Everybody all right?"

A chorus of voices cried: "Yes, thank you, Nurse Baker!"

"Good!" said Nurse Baker, and went back into the ward just as one of the porters entered.

"You 'aven't seen a little boy wearin' a red pullover, 'ave yer?" he asked.

"No," said Nurse Baker.

"I s'pose 'e might be in the playroom," said the porter.

"I've just been in there," said Nurse Baker, "and there's certainly no one in a red pullover."

"Ah well, 'e must be somewhere else," said the porter.

Jeremy James and Simon had an interesting telephone conversation. Simon told Jeremy James that he'd just had his tonsils out, and it was very painful but everyone had said how brave he was, and he'd be going home tomorrow. Jeremy James told Simon that he'd broken his wrist catching a bank robber, and everyone had said he was a hero, and he was going to have an egg-ray to see if his hand might drop off.

By now the hospital authorities had decided that the police must be brought in, and at exactly the same moment that Jeremy James was telling Simon how he'd ... well ... *almost* caught the bank robber, Mummy was giving a policeman a detailed description of Jeremy James. Another policeman was talking to the old lady who'd seen the boy with the man in the overalls. Someone else had also seen them, and the boy had been wearing a brown jacket, had swung his left arm, and had called the man Daddy.

"Then maybe he was a different boy," said the old lady.

Jeremy James might well have stayed in the playroom for the rest of the day, and maybe even the night as well, if at that moment Simon's mummy and daddy hadn't happened to come in to see their son. First they said hello to Simon, and then they said hello to his new friend, and when they asked the new friend what his name was, Simon's mummy said:

"Isn't that the little boy they're all looking for?"

"Can't be," said Simon's daddy. "He's supposed to be wearing a red pullover."

"*I've* got a red pullover," said Jeremy James, and pulled it out from under the chair to show them.

"Then you're the one they're looking for," said Simon's daddy.

There was quite a lot of fuss when Jeremy James was finally taken back to see Mummy and the twins. Mummy threw her arms round him as if he'd really caught the bank robber, the rosy-cheeked nurse and the pigtailed lady were in tears, the grey-haired receptionist was smiling, two doctors and two policemen were frowning, and Jennifer was laughing, and Christopher was crying.

Jeremy James found it all rather puzzling, and told Mummy about the fish-tank and the fruit cake and the toy telephones.

One of the policemen took notes, and murmured

as he wrote: "Fish-tank . . . fruit cake . . . toy telephones . . . Crime o' the century."

Eventually, the policemen said goodbye, the doctors and nurses went back to work, and Jeremy James walked with his right hand in the hand of the pigtailed lady all the way to the X-Ray room. And when she'd finished taking the X-Ray, she held his hand all the way back to the waiting-room.

It turned out that Jeremy James had been right all along. His wrist wasn't broken. The doctor with the thinning red hair and the now-not-quite-so-twinkling blue eyes said it was just a sprain, and the now-extremely-rosy-cheeked nurse put a bandage on it.

There were more goodbyes, and at last Mummy, Jeremy James and the twins slowly made their way towards the big glass doors that self-opened and self-closed. But before they got there, Jeremy James stopped and looked up at Mummy.

"Mummy," he said.

"What is it, Jeremy James?" asked Mummy.

"Before we leave, please can we see the fish-tank?"

"No!" said Mummy.

Jeremy James couldn't understand why Mummy said it so sharply.

CHAPTER TWO

The Greatest Game

"I've been to lots of hospitals," said Timothy. "I've been to lots more hospitals than you'll ever go to."

"Well I've only ever been to one," said Jeremy James.

"And I've been to lots," said Timothy.

Timothy was the red-haired, freckle-faced boy from the big house next door, and he had not only been everywhere, but he had also done everything and knew everyone.

"What's the matter with you, then?" asked Jeremy James.

"Nothing's the matter with me," said Timothy. "I'm perfect."

"But people only go to hospital if they're ill," said Jeremy James. "Like me, with my pained wrist."

"I've had lots of pained wrists," said Timothy.

"You can't have lots," said Jeremy James, "because you've only got two wrists."

"I've had lots," said Timothy. "And I've had bigger bandages than that. I've had bandages all over my hand *and* my arm."

They were sitting on the lawn in the back garden, not far from the spot where yesterday Jeremy James had fallen off his tricycle. Timothy had come round to play, and although Jeremy James didn't really want to play with him, Mummy had said he should go and get some fresh air. Only he mustn't play any rough games like Cowboys and Indians because he had to be careful not to bump his wrist.

"A pained wrist never stopped *me* from playing Cowboys and Indians," said Timothy.

"Well, I had to have an egg-ray," said Jeremy James. "To see if my wrist was broken."

"It's not an egg-ray, it's an X-Ray. You don't know anything."

"Yes, I do, and I only had to have *one*, so it's an egg-ray."

Timothy pulled his six-shooter out of his holster and aimed it straight at Jeremy James's head.

"I've had lots of X-Rays, and I never cried once, and I played Cowboys and Indians straight after."

"I didn't cry," said Jeremy James. "Except just a bit."

"I'll bet you cried a lot," said Timothy. "Bang!"

A little puff of smoke came from the gun, as Timothy fired it.

"I only cried a tiny bit," said Jeremy James, "and I didn't cry at all in the hospital."

"Anybody can not cry in the hospital," said Timothy. "But I'll bet you cried buckets when you fell off your tricycle, and you should lie down dead 'cos I've just shot you."

But Jeremy James didn't feel like lying down dead, and he didn't feel like playing Cowboys and Indians with Timothy, because Cowboys and Indians *always* ended with him lying down dead. And in any case, Mummy had said he mustn't.

"You don't have to do what your Mummy says," scoffed Timothy. "I never do. In my house I do what *I* say."

"You don't always," said Jeremy James, "because when your Mummy calls you to come in for tea, you do what *she* says."

"That's only because I want to. I don't do what she says if I don't want to."

"Well I don't want to play Cowboys and Indians," said Jeremy James.

"Then what *do* you want to play?"

"Nothing."

Jeremy James hoped that Timothy would say "All right, I'm going home", but instead Timothy tore out a few handfuls of grass, tried to punch a passing fly, and then lay on his back and pedalled with his legs.

Just then, Timothy's mother poked her head over the garden fence.

"Hello, darlings!" she cried. "Are you having a lovely game?"

"No," said Timothy.

"Oh, and what's poor Jeremy done to his little hand, then?"

Mrs Smyth-Fortescue never called him Jeremy James, and Jeremy James never called her Mrs Smyth-Fortescue.

"Hello, Mrs Might-Forceapo," he said. "I've pained my wrist."

"Oh dear," said Mrs Smyth-Fortescue, "that must have been painful."

"No it wasn't," said Timothy. "But he cried all the same. I never cry when I pain my wrist, do I?"

"I don't think you've ever sprained your wrist, darling."

"Yes I have, lots of times."

"I don't think so, dear."

"Yes I have."

When they finished discussing whether Timothy

had or had not sprained his wrist, Mrs Smyth-Fortescue announced that she was driving into town, and Timothy should come with her. A smile came to Jeremy James's face.

"No, I'll stay here and play with Jeremy James," announced Timothy, and the smile left Jeremy James's face.

"All right then, dear," said Mrs Smyth-Fortescue. "Since you're both getting along so well. Jeremy, just run and ask your Mummy if it'll be all right. Tell her I'll only be an hour or two."

"An hour or two!" cried Jeremy James. "But that's hours and hours!"

"Run along and ask your Mummy, dear."

Jeremy James ran along and asked his Mummy. He said, "Mummy, it won't be all right for Timothy to stay here for hours and hours, will it?"

But Mummy said it would. In fact, she said it twice, because Jeremy James asked her twice.

Fortunately, Daddy decided that he'd had enough of thinking about planning to start trying to get down to doing some work, and came out into the garden with Jeremy James.

When Mrs Smyth-Fortescue had gone ("Dear Timothy won't be any trouble. The boys do get on so nicely, don't they?"), Daddy suggested a game of I-Spy.

"I-Spy's for little kids," said Timothy.

"Ah!" said Daddy. "Well, how about hide-and-seek?"

"Your garden's not big enough for hide-and-seek," said Timothy.

"Ah!" said Daddy. "How about blind man's buff?"

"Boring!" said Timothy.

"Hunt the thimble?"

"Boring!"

Daddy mentioned a game that Jeremy James had never heard of, called "Kill Your Neighbour", but Timothy wanted to play nothing except Cowboys and Indians.

"I'll be the cowboy," he said, "because I've got the gun, and you can be the Indians and I'll shoot you."

"What fun!" said Daddy. "No, I've got a better idea. We'll play football."

"I don't like football," said Timothy.

"Hold on, hold on," said Daddy. "Not ordinary football – too dangerous for Jeremy James. I'll be in goal, and you two can take it in turns to try and score."

"Boring," said Timothy.

"And whoever scores the most goals wins a bar of chocolate," said Daddy.

Timothy, who had just opened his mouth to say "boring", left his mouth open for a moment, and then murmured, "bar of chocolate". A bar of chocolate wasn't boring. A bar of chocolate was even worth playing football for.

"We'll play for twenty minutes," said Daddy.

'And I'll take the first kick," said Timothy.

"All right," said Daddy, "but that means Jeremy James takes the last kick."

Daddy fetched Jeremy James's football, and went and stood in front of the shed (at the side without a window). Then he rolled the ball gently towards Timothy.

Timothy's first shot missed the shed altogether and flew into the vegetable patch.

"Goal!" shouted Timothy.

"What do you mean, goal?" said Daddy. "You missed!"

"You didn't stop it," said Timothy, "so it's a goal."

Daddy explained that the ball had to hit the shed, and Timothy said it didn't. If the ball beat the goal-keeper, said Timothy, it was a goal, because those were the rules, and he knew because he'd seen real football on television, and that was how it was played.

"The ball goes into a net in real football," said Daddy. "But as we haven't got a net, we're going to use the side of the shed, and this is our garden, and those are the rules in our garden."

"Well I didn't know that," grumbled Timothy, "and it's not fair, 'cos I would have kicked the ball at the shed if—"

"Right, start again," said Daddy.

Timothy ran up and gave the ball an almighty kick, but the ball went straight into Daddy's tummy. Daddy said "Ouf!" as he caught it, and then he rolled it towards Jeremy James.

Jeremy James didn't kick the ball nearly as hard as Timothy had done, but it also went straight towards Daddy. As Daddy bent down to stop it, though, he slipped, and somehow the ball managed to roll under his body and hit the shed.

"Goal!" shouted Jeremy James.

"That's not fair!" shouted Timothy. "You stopped *my* ball, and you let Jeremy James's ball hit the shed."

"Terrible mistake," said Daddy. "What a blunder. One nil to Jeremy James."

For his next kick, Timothy dribbled the ball up to within a couple of yards of the shed.

"Hold on, you can't do—" said Daddy, but before he could say what Timothy couldn't do, Timothy showed just what he could do. The ball crashed into the side of the shed like an exploding shell.

"One all," said Timothy.

"Hmmph," said Daddy. "Good shot, Timothy, but you're not allowed to come that close."

"Yes I am," said Timothy. "I can come as close as I like."

"Not in our garden," said Daddy again, and took several paces across the lawn before drawing a line with the heel of his shoe.

"You can't come beyond this line," he said. "Either of you."

"It's one all," said Timothy.

"All right," said Daddy. "One all."

"That's not fair," said Jeremy James. "If Timothy

had a kick from that close, then I should have a kick too."

"True," said Daddy. "Just one."

And so Jeremy James came up to within a couple of yards of Daddy, and kicked the ball straight past him.

"Two one," shouted Jeremy James, and ran back waving his right arm to the sky.

From then on, the game got fiercer and fiercer. Daddy made some brilliant saves, especially from Timothy's thunderbolts, but he also made some awful mistakes. Once, when Timothy had actually drawn level, Daddy dived the wrong way to one of Jeremy James's shots, but another time, when Jeremy James was two goals ahead, he completely missed an easy one from Timothy. The score mounted up, and the minutes ticked away.

"Twelve eleven to Jeremy James," called Daddy, "and three minutes to go . . ."

The excitement was now almost too much to bear. The thousands of spectators that weren't watching would have been on their feet cheering every shot and every save. Timothy's face was as red as a Rovers' jersey, and he was running to take his shots as if the World Cup itself were the prize.

And then came the most dramatic moment of the most dramatic game in the whole history of world football. With thirty seconds to go, and the score at thirteen twelve to Jeremy James, Daddy accidentally kicked the ball right across the garden into the flower bed next to the fence. Timothy's legs were a whirl of pink as he ran after it. Then suddenly, as his toe made contact with a raised paving slab, the whirl turned into a sprawling dive, and down went Timothy in an untidy heap on the garden path.

Timothy's "Ouch" and "Owowow" were just like Jeremy James's the previous day, only twice as loud, and the wah-woos that followed were three times as loud as that. If the thousands of spectators who were not watching the football had been cheering now, they would not even have heard their own cheers, so loud were Timothy's wah-woos.

Daddy ran across the lawn, and Jeremy James followed.

"Where does it hurt?" asked Daddy.

"*Waaaah-woooo!*"

Jeremy James put his hands to his ears, as Timothy pointed deafeningly to his left leg.

Daddy very gently prised Timothy's hands away from the damaged leg, and uncovered a tiny graze from which came the thinnest trickle of blood.

"*Waaaaaah-woooooo!*"

"Is that it?" asked Daddy.

Timothy gave an ear-splitting nod.

"Well, we'll soon get that seen to," said Daddy, and he picked Timothy up in his arms and carried him towards the house.

Mummy had already opened the kitchen door, having noticed that the air outside had been suddenly ripped apart.

"What happened?" she asked.

"Our hero fell over," said Daddy, "and grazed his knee."

"*Waaaaaah-woooooo!*"

Mummy fetched some cotton wool and a bowl of water, and while Daddy sat Timothy on his knee, Mummy gently cleaned away the little blob of blood.

"*Waaaaaaaaah-wooooooooo!*"

When she had finished, Mummy stuck a little piece of plaster over the graze. Then slowly the storm subsided, the floods receded, and an uneasy calm settled over the kitchen, disturbed only by the occasional gurgling gulp.

"Are you all right now, Timothy?" asked Mummy.

Timothy nodded.

"Such courage!" said Daddy. "See if you can stand up."

Very carefully, Timothy put his right leg down on the floor, and then even more carefully lowered his left leg. Finally he allowed his whole body to follow, and stood quite still between Mummy and Daddy.

"Can you walk?" asked Mummy.

Timothy very carefully placed his right foot in front of his left and took a step forwards.

"That's wonderful," said Daddy. "A wonderful step, Timothy. Can you do another one?"

Timothy did another one.

"Extraordinary talent," said Daddy.

All this time, Jeremy James had been watching in silence, waiting to ask a vital question. Now he could wait no longer.

"Daddy," he said.

"Yes, Jeremy James?" said Daddy.

"Can I have my bar of chocolate?"

The question had a remarkable effect on Timothy. Suddenly, he seemed to forget completely about the terrible injury that had threatened to end his footballing career.

"It's not your bar of chocolate," he said.

"Yes it is," said Jeremy James.

"We didn't finish the game," said Timothy.

"I'm afraid you did," said Daddy. "The final

whistle blew while you were stroking the garden path with your knee."

"That's not fair," said Timothy. "I should have had another kick!"

But Daddy said it *was* fair, the twenty minutes had passed, Jeremy James had won thirteen twelve, and the referee's decision was final.

"You're not the referee," said Timothy, "you're the goalkeeper."

"But," said Daddy, "it's my garden."

With that he handed Jeremy James an unopened, silver-papered, blue-wrapped bar of fruit and nut.

"Now why don't you go outside," said Mummy, "and play a nice quiet game together till Timothy's mother gets home?"

Timothy limped out with a scowl, and Jeremy James walked out with a smile – and a bar of chocolate.

"It's not fair," said Timothy. "I should have won that chocolate."

"The only prize you should have won," said Jeremy James, slowly peeling the wrapper, "is a prize for crying."

"I wasn't crying," said Timothy, eyes fixed on the brown squares poking out of the silver paper. "I was just shouting a little."

"You cried so loud," said Jeremy James, snapping off a square and popping it in his mouth, "that I had to shut my ears."

"Ears can't be shut," said Timothy, "and can I have a bit?"

"No," said Jeremy James. "Because I won it, and because you said you didn't cry but you did."

Jeremy James broke off another square, and Timothy watched it disappear.

"If I say I did cry, will you give me a bit?" he asked.

Jeremy James thought for a moment.

"I'll give you a bit," he said, "if you say you cried a lot."

"Icralot," mumbled Timothy.

"Say it properly," said Jeremy James.

"I cried a lot," said Timothy.

By the time Timothy had said that he'd cried a lot, cried more than Jeremy James, cried like a baby, lost the football match, was a silly boy, and should have his bottom smacked, he and Jeremy James between them had finished the bar of chocolate. Jeremy James reckoned it was the best game he had ever played with Timothy.

"Hello, darlings!" said a familiar voice over the garden fence. "Mummy's back. Have you had a lovely time together?"

"Yes, thank you," said Jeremy James, at the same time as Timothy was saying "No."

"That's good!" said Mrs Smyth-Fortescue. "And you're such good boys, I've brought you back a little present."

She held her hands out over the fence, and in each hand was a blue-wrapped, silver-papered bar of fruit and nut.

"One for each of you," she said.

It really had been a very enjoyable afternoon.

CHAPTER THREE

Gran

Richard was the roly-poly boy who lived round the corner at No. 24. He had shiny cheeks, and Jeremy James always liked playing with him, because he was nice and kind and fun and not Timothy.

The only problem in Richard's house was Gran. She was very old and tiny and sort of dry, and she sat in the armchair all day sleeping. The only time she didn't sleep was when Richard and Jeremy James wanted to play a game. If it was a video game, she'd be wanting to watch something on the TV, and if it was any other sort of game, she'd wait till they were right in the middle of it, and then she'd think of something for Richard to do. There was always something for Richard to do. Richard reckoned she just sat there all day thinking up new things for him to do, and if there weren't any new things, she'd ask him to do the old things.

"Richard, dear," she'd say, "would yer fetch me book/pen/pencil/newspaper/purse/slippers/cushion/pills/powders . . ."

Or: "Would yer just pop round to the store and

buy me some apples/bread/milk/sugar/salt/vinegar/mustard/envelopes/stamps/pills/powders . . ."

Gran had a lot of pills and powders. She ate pills and powders like some people eat chocolate.

"Richard, dear, would yer just come and put this plug in/pull that plug out/post this letter/find me glasses/open the curtain/ close the window/switch on the radio/switch off the telly . . ."

Once she'd sent Richard to the library, and Jeremy James had gone with him. They'd taken Richard's gerbil, which had escaped and caused a lot of people to scream and jump on tables. That wouldn't have happened if Gran hadn't said, "Richard, would yer just pop round to the library and change me books."

The trouble was, Gran's legs were very bad. She was always saying how bad her legs were. "Oooh me legs are bad today," she'd say, and that meant she couldn't get up and do anything. And *that* meant Richard had to get up and do something.

It wouldn't have been quite such a problem if Richard's mum and dad didn't both go to work, but as they were out most of the day, it was Gran who looked after Richard. And *that* meant Richard looked after Gran.

On this particular day, Richard wanted to show Jeremy James his new tree-house, which his dad had built for him.

"Just going into the garden, Gran, to play in the tree-house," said Richard.

"All right, dear," said Gran.

Then as Richard opened the French windows, Gran said: "Oh, Richard, dear, before yer go, could yer just fetch me walkin' stick. It's in the hall."

"Yes, Gran," said Richard, and slipped out into the hall.

Jeremy James's eyes had opened wide. He'd never seen a stick walking before, and he waited eagerly for it to come striding through the door. He was a bit disappointed when Richard came back carrying it.

"Is your stick going to walk, Gran?" he asked.

"My stick walk?" repeated Gran. "No, of course it isn't."

"Then why's it called a walking stick?" asked Jeremy James.

Richard told Jeremy James that the stick was just supposed to help Gran to walk.

"It's because me legs are bad," said Gran. "Ooooh they are bad, specially today. This is a very bad day for me legs. Richard, dear, just help me get up from here, will yer?"

With a lot of oohing and aahing, she heaved herself out of the chair, with Richard and Jeremy James pulling and pushing. Then she took the stick in her hand, and leaned on it.

It was the first time Jeremy James had ever seen Gran get out of the chair. He'd always thought she lived in it.

"Are you coming to the tree-house with us?" he asked.

"No, dear," said Gran. "Can't do the climbin'. It's me legs, yer see. Can't climb trees with me legs."

"Perhaps you could use your hands," said Jeremy James.

"Then what would I hold me stick with?" asked Gran.

Jeremy James watched as she took a couple of shaky steps across the room.

"Your stick isn't very good, is it?" said Jeremy James.

"Isn't it?" asked Gran.

"Not if it's supposed to help you walk," said Jeremy James. "I can walk a lot better than that *without* a stick."

37

"Ah yes," said Gran, "but then you haven't got my legs, have yer?"

Jeremy James wouldn't have wanted Gran's legs. He much preferred his own.

"Can we go now, Gran?" asked Richard.

"Yes, off yer go," said Gran.

But just as Richard and Jeremy James were heading again for the garden, she said: "Oh Richard, dear, before yer go, could yer just slip into the hall an' open the lavatory door for me. Yer know how it sticks."

"Ye-e-es, Gra-a-an," said Richard, and slipped out into the hall.

"If your Gran sits down on the lavatory," said Jeremy James, when Richard had come back, "she might never get up again."

"I know," said Richard. "I hope she doesn't ask me to help her up from *there*."

To get to the tree-house, they had to climb a wooden ladder. Richard climbed it very slowly and huffily-puffily, sounding a bit like Gran getting out of her chair. Jeremy James (whose wrist was quite better now) pretended he was a fireman, and blazed his way to the top. Once they were up there, it was exciting to look round at the branches and look up at the sky and look down at the grass. You could imagine you were a lion or a tiger resting there.

The house itself was a platform in the fork of the tree, and it was all fenced in so that you couldn't fall off. Richard had a waterproof box with some toys in

38

it, and toys in a tree were a lot more interesting than toys on the ground. A little racing car, for instance, went skidding across the platform, under the fence, and crashing down to the grass below. You couldn't do that on the ground. And fishing with a magnetic rod was six times more fun when the fish were six foot below than when they were just lying on the carpet. And when a brown speckled bird landed on a branch two feet away and dropped a splashy white splodge on to the lawn, the two boys simply howled with laughter.

"Why don't we have tea up here?" suggested Richard, two hours before tea-time.

"Good idea," said Jeremy James, who was ready for tea at any time.

Richard's Mum had left sandwiches and cakes for them in the kitchen, and so Jeremy James the fireman hot-footed it down the ladder. Richard then lowered himself hippopotamously, rung by rung.

"I hope Gran's asleep," whispered Richard. "Let's tiptoe through the living-room."

But Gran wasn't asleep. Gran wasn't in the living-room at all.

"That's funny," said Richard. "I wonder where she is."

They didn't have to wonder long.

"Richard!" came a muffled voice. "Richard, where are you?"

"I'm here, Gran," cried Richard. "Where are *you*?"

"I'm in the lavatory, dear! I can't get out."

Richard and Jeremy James hurried into the hall.

"The door's jammed," said Gran from inside the lavatory. "See if you can open it."

Richard tugged the handle, but the door didn't move. Jeremy James again tugged the handle, and again the door didn't move.

"You'll have ter get some help," said Gran. "Fetch the fire brigade."

Jeremy James didn't think the fire brigade would be much help, unless Gran was to start a fire in the lavatory. But it did give him an idea. He himself had once been locked in the bathroom, and Daddy had climbed up a ladder and crawled through the window to rescue him.

"Is there a window in the lavatory?" he asked Richard.

Richard said there was, and so the two boys went outside to have a look at it. There was quite a big square window which couldn't be opened, but above that was a little one which *was* open.

"We can climb through that and rescue Gran!" said Jeremy James.

"*I* can't climb through that!" said Richard. "I'd get stuck."

"Well I can," said Jeremy James.

"Where are yer?" cried Gran. "What yer doin'?"

"We're outside, Gran," said Jeremy James, "and we're going to rescue you."

"Fetch the fire brigade!" cried Gran.

Jeremy James remembered what Daddy had said to him when he'd been locked in.

"Keep calm, Gran," he said. "Nothing to worry about. We'll soon get you out of there."

"How are you going to climb up?" asked Richard.

"The tree-house ladder," said Jeremy James. "Come and help me carry it."

And so with a few more reassuring words to Gran, they went back into the house, through the living-room, out into the garden, and across to the tree-house. Then together, they tipped the ladder on to its side and, like a pair of hi-ho window-cleaners, marched back across the garden, round the side of the house, and up to the lavatory window. Then they stood the ladder on end, and Jeremy James climbed to the top and peeped through the open window. Gran was sitting on the lavatory.

"What yer doin'?" asked Gran looking up at Jeremy James looking down.

"What are *you* doing?" asked Jeremy James. He certainly didn't want to climb through the window if Gran was still doing what she'd gone to do in the first place.

"I'm sittin' here waitin' fer the fire brigade," said Gran.

"Have you finished doing your Number Two?" asked Jeremy James.

Gran said she'd been in there long enough to finish a hundred and fifty Number Twos, and – as Jeremy James poked his head, shoulders and arms through

42

the narrow gap – what did he think *he* was doing?

Jeremy James said he was coming in, and before Gran could even begin to heave herself off the lavatory seat, he'd come tumbling down over the window-sill, past the sink, and on to the floor at her feet.

"Ouch!" said Jeremy James. "Owowow!"

"Oooh!" said Gran. "Owowoooh!"

"I've hurt my wrist!" said Jeremy James.

"You've hurt me leg!" said Gran. "The bad one. The really bad one. Both me legs are bad, but you've hurt the really bad one."

Jeremy James picked himself up and felt his left wrist. It was painful. He could feel the pain climbing into his eyes, but he made it go down again. Heroes rescue Grans before they cry.

"What's happening?" called Richard from the foot of the ladder outside.

"It's all right," shouted Jeremy James.

And everything would have been all right if it hadn't been for one small detail that Jeremy James had not thought about before. Now that he'd got into the lavatory, how were he and Gran going to get out?

He pushed the door, but it wouldn't open. Then he hit it with his right hand, rammed it with his right foot, shoved it with his shoulder, knocked it with his knee, hammered it with his hip, and banged it with his bottom. But still the door wouldn't open.

"Richard!" called Gran.

"Yes, Gran?" called Richard.

"Go an' see if there's anyone next door!"

"All right, Gran."

There was a long silence. Gran sat on the seat, holding her walking stick, and Jeremy James stood at the door holding his wrist.

"Are you there, Gran?" came Richard's voice eventually.

"Course I'm here!" said Gran. "Well?"

"There *is* somebody next door," said Richard. "I saw Mr Biddle in his living-room. He's watching cricket on TV."

"Is he comin'?" asked Gran.

"No," said Richard.

"Why not?" asked Gran.

"'Cos he's in his living-room," said Richard.

44

"Did yer tell him we were stuck in here?" asked Gran.

"No," said Richard. "You just told me to see if anyone was there."

Gran groaned and told Richard to fetch Mr Biddle. A few minutes later Mr Biddle arrived, pulled open the lavatory door ("Ah, it's the spinkle-hasket-toggle-brock!") and Gran and Jeremy James came out into the hall.

"Are you all right, Gran?" asked Mr Biddle.

"Yes, thanks very much, Mr Biddle," said Gran. "I'm all right. It's just me legs, yer know."

"Are you all right, Jeremy James?" asked Richard.

But Jeremy James was not all right. His wrist hurt. A lot.

"I think I've pained it," he said with a screwed-up voice.

Mr Biddle hurried back to his living-room ("England need me," he said), Gran went to the kitchen to make herself a cup of tea, and Jeremy James went home to have his wrist seen to. The last thing he heard as he left Richard's house was the voice of Gran:

"Richard, dear, would yer just get me some milk."

CHAPTER FOUR

The Parcel

Daddy had gone into town, and everybody else was relaxing in the garden. Mummy and the twins were asleep in the shade of the apple tree, and Jeremy James was thinking that it was time for some chocolate.

The more Jeremy James thought about his chocolate, the more he needed it. His mouth ached for the bite-chew-yumminess of the fruit and nut bar he had put on the top shelf of the fridge. It seemed to be calling him. "Come and get me!" it was saying. "I'm so lonely in here! Jeremy James! Jeremy James! Come and eat me!"

Jeremy James could ignore the call no longer. Taking care not to disturb Mummy, he padded across the lawn and into the kitchen. There he opened the fridge door, and took out the blue-wrapped bar of heavenly delight. He held it tenderly in his bandaged left hand, and with his expert chocolate-breaking right hand was just about to peel and snap when . . .

DING-DONG!

That was the front doorbell. Jeremy James was so

46

surprised that he dropped the chocolate on the floor. The DING-DONG had sounded almost like CAUGHT YOU, although it was *his* chocolate, and he wasn't doing anything naughty.

He picked up the bar, put it back in the fridge, and hurried to the front door. And there stood a small round-shaped postman carrying a large square-shaped packet.

"Parcel for you," he said. "Can you manage? It's a bit heavy."

Jeremy James took the parcel. It *was* heavy, but he held it tightly against his chest.

"Yes, thank you," he said.

The postman closed the front door for him, and he carried the parcel into the living-room, where he managed to lift it up on to the table. Then he climbed on to a chair, and had a good look. (For some reason the chocolate had now stopped calling.)

It was an interesting parcel. It was box-like, wrapped in brown paper, tied up with string, and had various labels on it, including some red ones. These contained one word, but although he could read the letters – F-R-A-G-I-L-E – he didn't know the word they spelt.

Now a box like that could hold any number of things. A hundred bars of chocolate to start with. Or maybe toys. Or books. Or clothes. Chocolate and sweets would be best. Clothes would be worst.

Jeremy James grasped the parcel in both hands and shook it. There was just a slight rattle, but it wasn't a sound you could definitely say belonged to chocolate, toys or books. On the other hand, clothes wouldn't make any sort of rattle, because clothes were soft. Good.

A parcel like that really needed to be opened quickly. If it *was* chocolate, it could easily melt. Now that would be – as Daddy said once when his football team lost in the last minute – a tragedy.

Jeremy James climbed down from the chair, and ran out into the garden to the apple tree. Mummy was still fast asleep.

"Jem Jem!" said Jennifer, climbing to her feet in the play-pen, and smiling broadly. "Play with Jeffer?"

"I'm busy," said Jeremy James. "There's a parcel. A very important parcel."

He looked at Mummy, hoping she'd heard, but she hadn't.

"Parcel!" said Jennifer. "Portant parcel."

"It's got to be opened," said Jeremy James. "Before it melts."

But still Mummy remained stubbornly asleep.

"Melts!" said Jennifer. "Choc-let." (Like her elder brother, Jennifer was an expert on this subject.)

"That's right!" said Jeremy James.

Christopher now scrambled to his feet.

"Choc-let!" he cried. "Where?"

"It's in the parcel!" said Jeremy James.

"Here!" cried Jennifer. "Choc-let here!"

Jeremy James again looked at Mummy, but despite the excitement and the urgency of her children's needs, she was still unwakably asleep.

"It might not be chocolate," said Jeremy James. "It could be toys, or books, or clothes."

"Choc-let!" said Jennifer.

"Choc-let!" said Christopher.

It just had to be chocolate, since everybody wanted it to be chocolate, but how long would it stay chocolate? If it wasn't opened soon, it would turn into brown liquid, and then it would start dripping through the paper all over the table, all over the living-room, all over the house. The house would be flooded. Mind you, a house flooded with chocolate could be fun . . . But Mummy and Daddy wouldn't like it, would they? They'd say, "Jeremy James, why didn't you open the parcel and put the chocolate in the fridge, before it melted?" He could hear them saying it.

Jeremy James went back into the house, and climbed on to the chair again. Then he picked up the parcel and examined it for dripping brown stains. There were none, but again the box gave a little rattle. Maybe it was sweets after all. But sweets could melt too. Anything could melt in this heat.

Jeremy James climbed down and went into the kitchen. He picked up the scissors from the kitchen table, and returned to the living-room. With two big snips he cut the string, and then with a few more snips and rips he removed all the brown paper, revealing a cardboard box which was sealed with brown tape. Snip, rip, and away came the brown tape, and the box was ready for opening.

Jeremy James lifted the lid, and found that the box was full of soft paper. It wasn't chocolate-wrapping paper. It wasn't even sweet-wrapping paper. It was nothing-wrapping paper. He took it out, and put it on the table. Ah! There was something in the middle of the box – something hard, though it was wrapped in something soft. The something soft was a sort of bubbly material. Jeremy James lifted the whole thing out of the box, which he pushed aside with his elbow, and set it down on the table in front of him.

It certainly wasn't chocolate. Or sweets, or toys, or books, or clothes. It was something solid, and it wasn't melting, and there was just one of it, and it was heavy, and it was a funny shape, and it rattled a bit. So what was it?

There was only one way to find out. Mummy and Daddy would still be pleased with him if he had saved them the trouble of undoing the parcel, opening the box, and taking all the wrapping paper out. That was a lot of work, and Mummy and Daddy were always saying what a lot of work they had. Well, they wouldn't have to do this work. Jeremy James was doing it for them.

With a few more snips, he cut away the bubbly material, and came to a piece of gold-coloured metal. The metal was loosely attached to some glass, and as the rest of the bubbly material fell away, there lay the mystery object: a sort of pear-shaped lump of glass with a rattly piece of metal on it. Anything more unchocolate, unsweet, untoy, unbook, or even unclothing it was hard to imagine.

"What is it?" Jeremy James asked himself aloud.

Maybe the other side might be more interesting. Jeremy James picked it up to see.

And then something terrible happened. In order to do all the work that Mummy and Daddy now wouldn't have to do, Jeremy James had stood on the chair beside the table. But as he picked up the strange lump of glass, the chair seemed to slip away from him, and Jeremy James slipped with it, and the strange lump of glass slipped with Jeremy James, and all of them – chair, Jeremy James, and lump of glass – went crashing down to the floor below.

"Ouch!" cried Jeremy James. "Owowow!"

"Thump!" went the chair.

And "Crash-tinkle-splinter!" went the lump of glass.

Jeremy James lay on the floor, wondering which parts of his body were going to start hurting. One of them in particular was quick to send him a message: it was the one with a bandage on it.

"Owowow!" said Jeremy James again.

"What's happened? Oh good heavens, what's all this glass?"

Mummy, startled out of her sleep by what sounded like a bomb in the living-room, had come rushing in from the garden.

"Jeremy James, are you all right? Where did all this glass come from?"

Jeremy James thought of explaining to Mummy about the melting chocolate and the house being flooded, but he had a feeling that a few tears might be more use to him at the moment than a few words of explanation. Besides, his wrist really did hurt. It hurt enough for him to cry real tears.

When Daddy came home from town, he found the whole family out in the garden under the apple tree. Mummy was reading, Jeremy James looked as if he'd been crying, and the twins were playing quietly in their play-pen.

"Dad-dy!" cried Jennifer as he crossed the lawn.

Daddy bent down to kiss Mummy.

"Jem-Jem nor-ty!" said Jennifer.

"What's that?" asked Daddy.

Mummy explained that Jeremy James had opened a parcel containing the beautiful and very expensive lamp that she and Daddy had ordered from the beautiful and very expensive lamp shop in Castlebury two weeks ago.

"Ah!" said Daddy. "I was wondering when that would come."

"It came this afternoon," said Mummy.

"Good," said Daddy.

"It also went this afternoon," said Mummy.

"What do you mean?" asked Daddy.

"You'd better ask Jeremy James," said Mummy.

Daddy did ask Jeremy James. And Jeremy James explained, through a new trickle of tears, all about melting chocolate, and the house being flooded, and saving Mummy and Daddy lots of work, and . . .

"You dropped it," said Daddy.

"Yes," said Jeremy James.

He also told Daddy how he'd pained his wrist again, and Daddy said that maybe he ought to pain Jeremy James's bottom.

"You shouldn't go opening parcels, should you?" he said.

Jeremy James agreed.

"You could have had a really nasty accident, and fallen on some broken glass."

Jeremy James agreed.

"And even if it had been chocolate, it wouldn't have been *your* chocolate, would it?"

Jeremy James agreed.

"Let that be a lesson to you. No more parcel opening, right?"

Jeremy James agreed.

Then Mummy said maybe they should all go in and have some tea, and everyone agreed.

Two weeks later, Jeremy James happened to be playing with his racing cars when the postman rang. It was another heavy parcel, just like the first one. Jeremy James got the postman to put it down, and he went and told Daddy, who was in his study.

"It's a heavy parcel, like the first one!" said Jeremy James, and followed Daddy into the hall.

"It is indeed," said Daddy, picking it up. "But this time we shall make light of it."

Carefully Daddy carried the parcel into the living-room, and put it on the table.

"Now then, Jeremy James," he said, "let's show you how to open a parcel."

He snipped the string, snip-ripped the brown paper and the parcel tape, and opened the box. Then he took out all the wrapping paper, removed the bubbly material, and triumphantly lifted up the beautiful and very expensive glass lamp.

"And that, Jeremy James," he said, "is how you open a parcel without breaking the contents."

As he said it, he turned away from the table, and his right foot landed on Jeremy James's blue racing car. The car and the foot both skidded forwards, while the rest of Daddy seemed to go backwards, and the next moment his bottom hit the living-room carpet with a dull thump. Meanwhile, the lamp had jumped high in the air, and fallen to the floor with a loud and shattering and all-too-familiar crash.

After that, Mummy and Daddy decided it would be best to keep the old lamp for the time being. And Jeremy James agreed.

CHAPTER FIVE

Chocolate

"You're eating far too many sweets," said Mummy. "It's sweets and chocolate and cakes and ice cream all day long."

"I don't think it's too many," said Jeremy James. "I could eat a lot more."

"It's *far* too many," said Mummy. "And you've even got the twins at it now."

"Choc-let!" said Jennifer in her high chair, speaking through a mouthful of banana.

"Choc-let!" said Christopher, losing a mouthful of banana from his high chair.

"There you are!" said Mummy. "Choc-let! Choc-let! Nothing but choc-let."

"Yes, please," said Jennifer.

The family were at the table, and just because Jeremy James hadn't been hungry for vegetable lasagne, Mummy had started to talk about sweets. It was true that Jeremy James had had a few sweets this morning, and a couple of squares of chocolate. Well, half a bar, actually, but it was only the half bar left over from the bar he'd started the previous night, and you should never leave things once you've started them. But that wasn't the reason for his not being hungry for vegetable lasagne. He didn't like vegetable lasagne. Or at least he didn't like vegetable lasagne as much as he liked chocolate.

"At this rate," said Mummy, "you'll have no teeth by the time you're twenty."

Jeremy James frowned.

"Why won't I have any teeth?" he asked.

"They'll have rotted away," said Mummy. "Remember what Mr Pulham told you about the Tooth-Dragon?"

Mr Pulham was the dentist who'd killed a Tooth-Dragon in Jeremy James's mouth.

"Tooth-Dragons like sweet things," said Mummy. "That's what he told you."

"But Daddy eats chocolate," said Jeremy James.

"Choc-let!" said Jennifer.

"Choc-let!" said Christopher.

"Daddy doesn't eat as much as you," said Mummy. "And anyway, Daddy's giving it up."

Jeremy James looked wide-eyed at Daddy, and Daddy looked down at the table-cloth and nodded, a little sadly.

"It's true," he said. "The supreme sacrifice. No more chocolate."

"Choc-let!" cried Jennifer.

"Choc-let!" cried Christopher.

"What about sweets?" asked Jeremy James.

"Sweets!" cried Jennifer.

"Sweets!" cried Christopher.

"Sweets as well," said Daddy. "From now on, Jeremy James, we're going to eat nothing but healthy things like fresh fruit and vegetables. Then we'll both grow up to be big and strong. Like your mother."

Mummy laughed, but Jeremy James didn't think it was funny. Fruit and vegetables instead of sweets and chocolate was no joke. It was the same old story. Whatever you liked was bad for you, and you had to eat/drink/do what you didn't like to be a good boy. Did a grown-up ever ask you to give up vegetable lasagne? Or cabbage, or tomatoes, or oranges?

"Now finish your lasagne," said Mummy.

Jeremy James chewed the mouthful of lasagne that he'd been chewing since Mummy first mentioned chocolate. It was like chewing rubber.

"Why is rubber good for you and chocolate bad for you?" asked Jeremy James.

"What?" said Mummy.

"Bacteria," said Daddy.

Daddy always used long words when you asked him a difficult question. Mummy usually said "Hmmph", and Daddy usually said "Worple, worple semantics", but this time Daddy said "Bacteria".

"They're little tiny weeny creatures," said Daddy, "that love sugar. So if you get sugar on your teeth, they come along and eat your teeth. Or something like that."

"Well, if I kept my mouth closed," said Jeremy James, "they wouldn't be able to get in, would they?"

"If you kept your mouth closed," said Daddy, "the chocolate wouldn't be able to get in either."

"Choc-let!" squealed Jennifer.

"Choc-let!" squealed Christopher.

"I could put the chocolate in very quickly," said Jeremy James.

"Not quickly enough," said Daddy. "Besides, for all you know, the bacteria could be *in* the chocolate."

Jeremy James thought for a moment.

"If they're in the chocolate," he said, "why haven't they eaten it themselves?"

"It's all a matter of worple worple semantics," said Daddy.

Jeremy James reckoned it was all a matter of grown-ups not knowing what was good for little boys. And when afters turned out to be fresh fruit salad *without ice cream*, he knew that this would never again be home, sweet home.

During the weeks that followed, the family ate nothing but "healthy" food. That meant fruit, vegetables, fish, vegetables, fruit, salad, fruit, vegetables, wholemeal bread, vegetables, fruit, plain yoghurt, and fruit and vegetables.

One day Mummy announced that she had lost ten pounds. Jeremy James immediately offered to find it for her, but it turned out she meant weight and not money, and she was pleased with herself.

"It's all done by eating the right things," she said.

"Have I lost weight too, Mummy?" asked Jeremy James.

"I hope not," said Mummy. "We don't want *you* to get thinner."

"I *am* getting thinner," said Jeremy James, "so maybe I should eat some wrong things, and . . ."

But Mummy soon proved that Jeremy James was not getting thinner. She made him stand on the bathroom scales, and he was two pounds heavier than when he'd last stood on them. For some reason, this proved that healthy food was good for Mummy, because she lost weight, and good for Jeremy James because he gained weight. Jeremy James did suggest that maybe he'd gain even more weight if he ate wrong things, but Mummy just said "Hmmph" and they went downstairs again.

Two days later, Jeremy James developed a sore throat. It was only slightly sore, but Mummy had a look and thought the throat was rather red, so she made an appointment for Jeremy James to see Dr Bassett.

"I'll take him," said Daddy. "I could do with an outing. Might freshen me up a bit."

Jeremy James had seen Dr Bassett before, when he'd been taken ill with liquorice allsorts flu. Dr Bassett was the tallest man in the world, and even when he sat down, he was tall enough to be standing up.

"Hello, John. Hello, Jeremy James," he said, when they entered the surgery. "Don't tell me. Let me guess. It's allsortitis."

"Well no, it's not actually," said Daddy. "He's got a bit of a sore throat."

"Ah!" said Dr Bassett. "Swallowed the packet as well, did he? Come here, Jeremy James, and let's have a look."

He got Jeremy James to open his mouth, and then he shone a little torch inside.

"Well now, old chap," he said, "what you've got there is a touch of tonsillitis. Bit of inflammation. Nothing serious. I'll give you some antibiotics."

Jeremy James didn't know what tonsillitis or inflammation were, but he knew what he hoped antibiotics were.

"Are they like liquorice allsorts?" he asked.

"What?" asked Dr Bassett.

"Antibottics," said Jeremy James.

"Afraid not," said Dr Bassett. "They're just pills to make your throat better. You've got some bacteria in there, so we'll try to kill them off. Right?"

Jeremy James's eyes opened wide.

"Bacteria?" he cried.

Dr Bassett looked surprised. "You know what they are?" he asked.

"They're tiny things that like sugar," said Jeremy James.

"Clever lad!" said Dr Bassett.

"But I haven't had any sugar," said Jeremy James. "Because I haven't had any sweets. I've only had fruit and vegibles and fish and yoghurt and brown bread."

Dr Bassett explained that bacteria were all over the place, and not just in sugar. Jeremy James asked if they were in vegetable lasagne.

63

"Could be," said Dr Bassett. "Who knows where the little devils hide themselves!"

Jeremy James found this very interesting, and he would have liked to ask some more questions. But what happened next was even more interesting. What happened next was the most interesting thing to have happened in all the weeks of sweetlessness.

Dr Bassett began to write on a piece of paper, and as he did so, he asked Daddy how *he* was.

"I'm fine, Robert, thanks," said Daddy. "Except that I seem to get very tired these days."

"So do I, John," said Dr Bassett. "So do I. Especially in the afternoons. Find myself nodding off in the middle of a diagnosis. You know what I do?"

Daddy shook his head. Dr Bassett reached out and opened a drawer, from which – with a little flourish of his hand – he produced . . . a bar of chocolate.

"A few squares of this," he said, "and I can write ten prescriptions a minute."

"Chocolate!" cried Jeremy James.

Jennifer and Christopher would also have cried "Choc-let!" if they'd been there.

"Just ups the blood-sugar," said Dr Bassett. "Here, have a piece."

Daddy and Jeremy James each took the piece that was offered to them, and as their lips closed and their teeth sank into the firm square of taste-bud-tingling delight, a look of exquisite pleasure spread across their faces.

"Mmmm!" said Daddy.

"Mmmm!" said Jeremy James.

"It's just ordinary chocolate," said Dr Bassett.

"It may be ordinary to you," said Daddy, "but it's a feast for us, eh, Jeremy James?"

"Mmmm!" said Jeremy James.

There was a long family discussion that evening. Jeremy James told Mummy all about the bacteria, Daddy told Mummy all about blood-sugar, and Mummy told Daddy and Jeremy James all about healthy food (again).

"What's needed here," said Daddy, "is compromise."

"What's needed here," said Jeremy James, "is chocolate."

"Choc-let!" said Jennifer.

"Choc-let!" said Christopher.

It turned out, though, that by "compromise" Daddy actually meant chocolate. And sweets and ice cream and cakes. But not too many. That was the important thing. They could be eaten in small quantities, and Jeremy James must ask Mummy first. Daddy didn't have to ask Mummy first, and Mummy didn't have to ask anybody because she wasn't going to eat sweet things anyway. And the twins would only have what Mummy gave them. Daddy said that was fair, Jeremy James said that was fairly fair, and the twins said "Choc-let!"

The next day, Mummy announced a special treat for lunch. She brought in a cheese and broccoli quiche. Jeremy James (whose sore throat was now better) had hoped it might be chicken and chips, but Mummy didn't cook chips any more. Not healthy, she said. The quiche was nice, especially for someone who hadn't had a thing to eat since breakfast, but it was hardly a special treat.

"The special treat," said Mummy, "is for dessert."

And dessert turned out to be fresh fruit salad, *with ice cream*. Jeremy James enjoyed his second helping as much as his first, and even Mummy had a spoonful and said how nice it was.

"I'd forgotten how nice ice cream can be!" said Mummy.

"I hadn't!" said Jeremy James.

All the same, he was not allowed a third helping, and later that afternoon he was not allowed to eat any chocolate. At least, not until he happened to find Daddy munching a piece in the kitchen. Daddy explained that he was feeling a bit tired, and was just upping his blood-sugar.

"I'm tired, too," said Jeremy James.

Daddy grinned, broke off a square, and he and Jeremy James untired themselves together.

CHAPTER SIX

The Fortune-Teller

There was a funfair on Cannon Green. Daddy said he thought Jeremy James would enjoy that. Mummy said she thought Daddy would enjoy it, too.

"Roundabouts, dodgem-cars, games, prizes," said Daddy. "Just the thing for little boys."

"Not to mention big boys," said Mummy.

And so Daddy and Jeremy James drove to Cannon Green, parked the car, and made their way towards the blaring music, the flashing lights, and the huge turning wheel that you could see even from the car-park.

The fun actually started before you got to Cannon Green, because along the path were stalls selling sweets, chocolate, ice cream, candy floss, and all the things that used to be good until they became bad. Jeremy James had a huge whirl of pink candy floss, but Daddy gritted his teeth and stopped himself from buying a bar of chocolate. Then he ungritted his teeth, and bought one.

"It's a treat," he said.

The whole funfair was a treat. Jeremy James drove

a car on a roundabout, while Daddy sat beside him and got dizzy. Then Daddy drove a car on the dodgems, while Jeremy James sat beside him and got bumped. A long-haired young man with a short-haired girlfriend drove into them and laughed, but Daddy managed to bump them back, and then Daddy laughed.

Jeremy James won a paintbox when he chose a special ticket, and Daddy won nothing when he fired a gun at some tin soldiers and missed. Then they both went on the Giant Slide, and they would also have gone on the Big Wheel if Daddy hadn't said that big wheels were just roundabouts turned on their side, and roundabouts made him go green.

Instead, Daddy tried to win a Red Indian kit for Jeremy James by throwing darts at some playing cards. Unfortunately, he missed as many cards with the darts as he'd missed soldiers with the gun.

"If you was a Red Indian throwin' tomahawks," said the man in the booth, "they'd 'ave to evacuate the camp."

There were so many things to see, and so many things to do, and so many people and so much noise that Jeremy James's head was buzzing. He didn't mind the buzz, though, because it was exciting, but Daddy must have had a less exciting buzz, because he wanted to find somewhere a bit quieter.

"All this oompah-crash-taraa-ra-ra is giving me a headache," he shouted.

"Is that why you missed with the darts, Daddy?" shouted Jeremy James.

"Well ... hmmph ... hum ... worple worple," said Daddy.

They made their way towards a corner of Cannon Green where there seemed to be fewer people and less taraa-ra-ra, and it was there that Daddy spotted a caravan with a notice outside: MADAME CLARE VOYANT, FORTUNE-TELLER. Underneath these words was a picture of a very beautiful gypsy girl.

"Would you like to have your fortune told?" asked Daddy.

"Does that mean she'll tell me how much money I've got?" asked Jeremy James.

"No," said Daddy, "it means she'll tell you your future."

It seemed to Jeremy James that if his future was connected to a fortune, it would certainly be a good idea to see the gypsy. And so he and Daddy climbed the two steps, and stood before the open red curtain, peering into the darkness.

"Come in, me dears," said a cracked old voice, and in they went.

On the other side of the curtain sat a little old lady dressed in colourful gypsy clothes.

"We've come to see Madame Clare Voyant," said Daddy.

"Then yer've come ter the right place," said the lady. "Forchunes fer both of yer?"

"Yes, please."

"That'll be three pounds, then, dearie."

"Hm, forchunes for you too," said Daddy. "Isn't it half price for children?"

"No, it ain't," said the lady. "Children oughter be double price, 'cos they've got twice as much future."

"That's true," said Daddy, and then paid three pounds.

"This way then," said the old lady, closing the red curtain, and she led them at a hobble into the depths of the caravan.

There were curtains over all the windows, but in the dim light Jeremy James could see a lot of masks, plants, and ornaments on the walls. There was also a strange smell, as if something sweet was burning.

The noise from outside seemed a long way away now, and the new quietness was somehow heavy. It wasn't frightening, but it wasn't pleasant either. He was glad that he had hold of Daddy's hand.

The old lady led them to a table with a glass ball and some cards on it.

"Shoo!" she said, and a black cat jumped off the chair behind the table, then disappeared into the shadows.

"Now then," said the old lady, sitting down in its place, "which of yer's goin' ter be first?"

"Just a minute," said Daddy, as he and Jeremy James sat on the two chairs facing her. "We want to see Madame Clare Voyant."

"You *are* seein' 'er," said the old lady.

"You're not the lady in the picture!" said Jeremy James.

"Oh yes I am," said the old lady. "That's what the future c'n do to yer."

"Hmmph!" said Daddy. "Well, don't you think you ought to change the photo?"

"Whatchoo come for?" asked the old lady. "Ter see a pretty face or 'ave yer forchune told? 'Oo's first, then?"

"Jeremy James," said Daddy.

"Crystal, cards or 'and?"

Jeremy James looked at Daddy.

"Do you want the lady to see your future in the glass, in the cards, or in your hand?" asked Daddy.

Since Jeremy James couldn't see much future in

his hand or in the cards, he chose the glass ball.

Madame Clare then made some airy movements with her hand over the ball, and mumbled some words that sounded very like "Worple, worple semantics . . ."

"Aha!" she said. "Ah! Aha! Yes, right, hmmm . . . I see a fine young man, tall, good-lookin'."

"Where?" asked Jeremy James.

"In me crystal ball," answered Madame Clare.

Jeremy James stood up to have a closer look.

"I can't see anyone," he said.

"That's cos you 'aven't got the power," said Madame Clare. "You 'ave to 'ave special powers ter see inter the future. Now, this tall an' 'andsome young man . . . 'e's got an unusual name . . . Jem . . . Jemmy . . ."

"Jeremy James," said Jeremy James.

"Is that you? Well, I never! Special powers, see? 'Ow did I know your name?"

"Daddy said it."

"Oh! Well, I'm sure I never 'eard. Now stop interruptin'."

Once again Madame Clare passed her hands over the crystal ball, screwed up her wrinkles in a frown of concentration, and gazed intently into the future.

"You're goin' ter be very tall, an' very 'andsome."

"Will I be taller than Timothy?" asked Jeremy James.

"'Oo's Timofy?"

"The boy next door."

"Oh, you mean the Timofy next door. Yes, 'e's short compared ter you. Ugly. Dark 'air . . ."

"Timothy's got red hair."

"That's right, dark red. But I'm lookin' at you now. An' I see a big 'ouse wiv a big garden . . ."

"We've only got a small house with a small garden," said Jeremy James. "You must be looking at Timothy's house."

"It's your *future* 'ouse, my dear," said Madame Clare.

Jeremy James looked into the crystal ball like a boy looking for a missing liquorice allsort, but still he could see nothing.

"I see you writin'," said Madame Clare. "Yes . . . letters, exams, cheques, books . . ."

"Daddy writes books," said Jeremy James.

"Does 'e?" said Madame Clare. "Well, that's it, then. You're goin' ter write books an' be rich an' famous."

Jeremy James smiled up at Daddy, and Daddy smiled down at Jeremy James. Next, Madame Clare announced that according to the latest crystal news bulletin, Jeremy James would have a beautiful fair-haired wife and five beautiful children – three boys and two girls – and would live till the ripe old age of 85.

"An' if this don't 'appen like I say, Jeremy James, yer can come back 'ere 'an I'll give you yer money back."

It was now Daddy's turn, and he told Madame

Clare to read his future in his hand. She very quickly discovered that he was an author, and lived with his family in a small house with a small garden.

"Let's see now," she said, "other children . . . I'm tryin' ter see if you've got other children."

"Christopher and Jennifer!" said Jeremy James.

"That's right," said Madame Clare. "A boy and a girl. They're older than Jeremy James . . ."

"No they're not!" said Jeremy James.

"Younger, I mean," said Madame Clare. "An' Jeremy James is older than them. Is that right?"

"Yes," said Jeremy James.

Then Madame Clare went on to talk about Daddy's books, and a possible move, and success, and to beware of a man with glasses who had something to do with money ("Is he a bank manager?" asked Daddy), and . . .

Jeremy James had now stopped listening to Madame Clare and to Daddy's future. His attention had been caught by a movement in the shadows behind the old lady. Something dark and slinky was easing its way along the shelf above her head. It was the black cat.

Madame Clare looked at Daddy's upraised palm, Daddy looked at Madame Clare, Jeremy James looked at the black cat, and the black cat looked at the large, dragon-painted vase right in the middle of the shelf beneath which Madame Clare was sitting.

"Excuse me!" said Jeremy James.

76

"Ssh!" said Madame Clare. "I see somethin' unexpected . . ."

"But the—"

"Somethin' very valu'ble . . ."

"The cat—"

"An' it's comin' your way . . ."

At precisely that moment, the black cat brushed against the large, dragon-painted vase, which tilted, toppled, and fell down with a loud *bonk* straight on to Madame Clare's head. The *bonk* was followed by three different noises: one was a miaowling screech from the cat, the second was a howling scream from Madame Clare, and the third was a clattering crash as the vase fell to the floor.

"Me head!" cried Madame Clare. "An' me vase!"

"And me future," murmured Daddy.

Fortunately, Madame Clare wasn't badly hurt, but her vase, her precious, been-in-the-family-for-generations Chinese-or-was-it-Japanese vase, would never be a vase again. It lay in at least twenty-two and a half pieces on the floor at her feet.

"Didn't you know it was going to fall?" asked Jeremy James.

"'Ow would I know that?" asked Madame Clare.

"I thought you knew the future," said Jeremy James.

Madame Clare rubbed her head.

"Nobody could 'ave known *that* sort of future," she said.

"*I* did," said Jeremy James.

Soon afterwards, when Daddy had made quite sure that Madame Clare was all right, he and Jeremy James left the caravan, walked back through the hustling-bustling hurly-burly, and drove home.

That evening, Jeremy James could talk of nothing else but the fortune-teller, the crystal ball, the black cat, and the vase.

"She didn't know it was going to fall," he told Mummy. "But I did."

There was one important question that Jeremy James still wanted to know the answer to, and so when Mummy and Daddy tucked him up in bed, he asked it.

"Am I really going to write books and be rich and famous?"

"Well," said Daddy. "If you don't become famous through writing books, maybe you'll make your fortune as a fortune-teller."

Jeremy James was still thinking about that when, without his even knowing it, let alone predicting it, he fell asleep.

CHAPTER SEVEN

Heaven

The gerbils were dead. Daddy had bought them on the twins' first birthday, and so Jeremy James had christened them Wiffer and Jeffer. He'd loved to hold them, and to watch them chasing round their cage, burrowing in the sawdust, or treadling their wheel. But last night they had both been lying quietly, and this morning they were lying dead.

"What made them die?" asked Jeremy James through his tears.

"Difficult to say without a post-mortem," answered Daddy.

"Will the postman bring one?" asked Jeremy James.

"A post-mortem's an examination," said Daddy, "to find the cause of death."

Jeremy James didn't want to examine Wiffer and Jeffer. He didn't even want to look at them lying there so still and stiff in the corner of their cage.

There had been a death in the family before. Great-Great-Aunt Maud had died at the age of ninety-two, and Jeremy James had gone to her funeral. She had been put in a beautiful shiny box, which Jeremy James would have liked to keep his toys and sweets in. Only the grown-ups had wasted it by putting it in the ground and covering it up with earth.

"We'll just bury them, shall we?" said Daddy. "Somewhere nice in the garden."

"Will we put them in a box?" asked Jeremy James. "Like Great-Great-Aunt Maud?"

"Yes," said Daddy. "Maybe you can go and find one, while I get things ready."

Jeremy James remembered something else about Great-Great-Aunt Maud.

"Can we have a party afterwards as well?" he asked.

"I expect Mummy will let us have a few sandwiches and cakes," said Daddy.

It so happened that Mummy had already planned to make sandwiches and cakes, because the Reverend Cole was coming round to discuss the church fête.

"Maybe if you ask him nicely," said Mummy, "the Reverend Cole might give the gerbils a proper burial."

Jeremy James thought that was a good idea, and so off he went to look for a box, while Mummy made the sandwiches and cakes, and Daddy went out into the garden to dig a grave.

The box that Jeremy James chose was bright and cheerful. Great-Great-Aunt Maud had been buried in one that was heavy and shiny and dark, but she'd been very old, and so maybe she hadn't liked cheerful boxes. The gerbils would have one that was covered in different-coloured blobs, each of which was a pleasure to look at whether you were alive or dead. It was an empty liquorice allsort box.

The Reverend Cole was very old, too, though not as old or as dead as Great-Great-Aunt Maud. He walked with a hobble, and talked with a wobble, and he had accidentally dropped Christopher in the font during the twins' christening. Jeremy James remembered that day very well, because he had accidentally been the cause of the Reverend Cole accidentally dropping Christopher.

"Never heard of dead marbles," said the Reverend Cole.

"Not marbles," said Jeremy James. "Gerbils."

"Ah!" said the Reverend Cole. "Where are they, then?"

"Here," said Jeremy James, holding out the liquorice allsort box.

"Thank you," said the Reverend Cole. "My favourite sweets."

He took the box, opened the lid, and found himself looking at Wiffer and Jeffer.

"Aaaugh!" he cried, and promptly dropped the box on the floor. Wiffer and Jeffer fell out on to the carpet, while the Reverend Cole did a sort of hobble-jump backwards, bumped straight into the coffee table, and knocked off the teapot that Mummy had just put there.

"Aaaugh!" cried the Reverend Cole again, as hot

tea splashed over his leg and foot. Then he hobble-hopped to an armchair, and hobble-slumped into it.

"Oh dear!" said Mummy. "I'm ever so sorry."

She fetched a couple of cloths, and while she wiped the Reverend Cole's shoe and trouser-leg, Daddy mopped up the tea from the carpet. Meanwhile, Wiffer and Jeffer lay next to the liquorice allsort box, and Jeremy James stood looking at them, with tears dropping out of his eyes.

Eventually, Daddy put them back in their box, Mummy made some more tea, and the Reverend Cole patted Jeremy James on the head.

"No harm done," he said. "Just a drop o' spilt tea. No need to cry."

Jeremy James hadn't been crying because of the spilt tea, but with Wiffer and Jeffer now safely back in their box, he stopped crying, and the Reverend Cole congratulated himself on his handling of the situation.

Daddy had dug a little grave under the apple tree, and very solemnly everyone trooped out into the garden. Mummy was holding Christopher, Daddy was holding Jennifer, Jeremy James was holding the box, and the Reverend Cole held forth:

"O Death," he said, "where is thy sting? O grave, where is thy victory? Oh Jeremy James, where is thy box?"

Jeremy James stepped forward with the box.

"Just put it in the . . . um . . . grave, will you?"

Jeremy James put the box in the grave.

"Forasmuch as the souls of these ... um ... gerbils here departed are in the care of Almighty God," said the Reverend Cole, "we therefore commit their bodies to the ground; earth to earth, ashes to ashes, dust to dust; in sure and certain ... um ... possible hope of eternal life, through our Lord Jesus Christ."

Beside the grave was a little pile of earth, which Daddy now pushed over the box until it was completely covered. Then the family went back into the house, and Mummy produced the sandwiches and cakes that were such an important part of any funeral.

"Will the gerbils be in Heaven now?" Jeremy James asked the Reverend Cole, through a mouthful of fruit cake.

"Ah!" said the Reverend Cole, through a mouthful

of salmon sandwich. "That's a very good question."

Since he showed no sign of answering it, Jeremy James asked him again.

"Many people do believe that animals have souls," he said, "and if they do, then I'm sure the gerbils will be in Heaven."

"What's a soul?" asked Jeremy James.

"It's the part of you that never dies," said the Reverend Cole. "It's your soul that goes to Heaven."

"Have I got one?" asked Jeremy James.

"Certainly," said the Reverend Cole.

"Where is it?" asked Jeremy James.

"Somewhere inside you," said the Reverend Cole.

Jeremy James would have liked to ask a lot more questions about his soul, but Mummy and the Reverend Cole had to talk about the fête, and so Jeremy James turned his thoughts to fruit cake instead.

That night, Jeremy James couldn't get to sleep. He was thinking about the gerbils and Heaven and his soul. He had asked Mummy and Daddy where his soul was, but their answer had been just as vague as the Reverend Cole's: "Hmmph" (Mummy) and "Worple worple" (Daddy).

He'd also asked them where Heaven was. Mummy thought it might be somewhere beyond the stars, and Daddy thought it was the football ground after a home win.

The problem for Jeremy James was that if the

Reverend Cole was right, and the soul was inside you, it would have to get out and find its way to Heaven. How could it do that if it didn't know – or if you didn't know – where Heaven was? Daddy, for instance, couldn't even find his way round London, so how would *he* get to Heaven?

"I expect someone comes to guide you," Mummy had said.

And that was keeping Jeremy James awake. Nobody had come to guide the gerbils. They'd simply been lying in their cage, then they'd been put in the liquorice allsort box, and buried under the apple tree. He would have *seen* if anyone had come to guide them.

Great-Great-Aunt Maud had been buried on a Saturday. Jeremy James remembered that very well, because Daddy had wanted to go to a football match, and on their way home, they'd had to drive through the crowd. But she hadn't died on the Saturday. She'd died before. So why hadn't she been buried on the day she died?

The answer was obvious. You had to wait till the guide had come before you put the body in the box and buried it. But the gerbils *had* been buried on the day they'd died. And now their souls would be trying to get out of the box and out of the ground before the guide came, because otherwise he'd never find them, would go away, and they would never get to Heaven.

Jeremy James reached for his torch, climbed out

of bed, put on his slippers, and opened the bedroom door. The whole house was dark and silent. Everyone was asleep.

Jeremy James crept downstairs, unbolted the kitchen door, and made his way across the lawn to the apple tree.

The following morning, when she looked out of the kitchen window, Mummy was surprised to see a brightly coloured box lying under the apple tree. She knew at once what it was, and when she went out to take a closer look, she found the lid open, and the two gerbils inside, just as dead as ever. She hastily closed the lid, put the box back in its hole, and covered it up.

"I suppose it must have been a dog," she said to Daddy when he came downstairs.

"I shouldn't think a dog would have left them lying there," said Daddy.

But neither of them could think of a better explanation, and they agreed not to tell Jeremy James, because they didn't want to upset him.

Jeremy James didn't wake up till quite late that morning, but as soon as he went downstairs, he wanted to go and look at the gerbils' grave.

"A good thing you spotted it," said Daddy to Mummy, when Jeremy James had gone. "Imagine what he'd have felt if he'd seen them lying there."

When Jeremy James returned, there was a big smile on his face.

"You're looking very pleased with yourself," said Daddy.

And Jeremy James *was* pleased with himself. He knew that the guide had come in the night and taken the gerbils (and the liquorice allsort box) to Heaven. But he decided not to tell Mummy and Daddy. They didn't know enough about souls or about Heaven to really understand.

CHAPTER EIGHT

The Fête

The church fête was on Saturday. From Monday to Friday, the sun shone and the sky was a cloudless blue. Then on Saturday it rained.

"Would you believe it?" said Mummy.

"Yes," said Daddy.

"But the weather forecast was for sunshine," said Mummy.

"Then we should have known it would rain," said Daddy.

Mummy had spent all Friday evening baking cakes to sell to people who hadn't heard that cakes were bad for them.

"I don't know what we're going to do with all these cakes if we don't sell them," she said.

Jeremy James knew what *he* would do with them, given half a chance. And he was sure Daddy and the twins would help him. He even offered to start straight away, but Mummy said, "We'll wait and see", which meant no.

Daddy carried the cakes through the wind and rain, and loaded them into the car ("They've all

turned into Bath buns," he said), while Jeremy James and the twins were wrapped up in their hooded anoraks. Then with Mummy carrying Christopher, Daddy carrying Jennifer, and Jeremy James carrying himself, they all made a splashing dash to the car.

"Jeffer wet!" announced Jennifer.

"Wiffer wet!" announced Christopher.

"Everybody wet," said Daddy. "They should have invited Noah to be guest of honour."

The guest of honour was in fact to be the Right Honourable Cecil Ponsonby-Thistlethwaite, MP, who – as Daddy explained to Jeremy James – was a politician.

Jeremy James had seen some politicians before, when Daddy had taken him to London.

"Is he one of those that's ruining the country?" he asked.

"He is indeed," said Daddy. "And if he makes a speech, he'll probably ruin the fête as well. If the rain hasn't ruined it already."

The rain was coming down harder than ever, and the wind was huffing and puffing like a pack of little-piggy wolves. The field was a thick and squelchy rug of mud, but someone had built a wooden pathway from the car-park to the big marquee, where the fête would now take place. Daddy carried the cakes, Mummy wheeled the twins in their push-chair, and Jeremy James hung on to Mummy's coat, as the wind blew them all the way to the marquee.

"Ah, there you are!" said the Reverend Cole. "What a day! The Lord must have got his dates mixed up!"

"Maybe He's telling us to cancel," said Daddy.

"No, no, we can't cancel," said the Reverend Cole. "The MP will be here soon."

"Maybe that's why the Lord wants us to cancel," said Daddy.

All round the marquee, people were setting up their stalls, and at one end there was a little platform on which a man in overalls was standing at a microphone. It kept making whistling and crackling noises, and the man kept saying, "Testing! Testing! Can you hear me?"

Daddy and Jeremy James both shouted yes.

"Thank you," said the man.

91

"Why does he want us to hear him?" asked Jeremy James.

"Because there's going to be a speech," said Daddy.

"Still testing," said the man. "Testing, testing."

"That's a boring speech," said Jeremy James.

Meanwhile, more people came trickling and dripping into the marquee, while the rain pounded against the roof, and the wind made the sides flap in and out as if they were taking deep breaths.

Suddenly there was a flurry of activity, as the Reverend Cole hurried like a lame tortoise towards a couple who had just come in. He arrived in time to take the man's hat and coat, and the lady's coat and umbrella.

The man was fat and bald, and wore a grey suit with a blue flower in the buttonhole. The lady was tall and thin, and wore a blue dress with white spots, and a white hat with blue spots. They made their way across the marquee, and as they came level with Jeremy James, the tall thin lady gave him a tall thin smile, and touched her husband's arm.

"Ah! A little boy," said the fat man. "Hello, little boy. How are you today?"

He really was very fat. His stomach was pressing hard against the closed buttons of his jacket, and Jeremy James wondered how far the buttons would go if they burst.

"Very well, thank you," said Jeremy James.

"Good," said the fat man. "You know who I am, don't you?"

"You're a Polly Tishun," said Jeremy James.

"That's right!" cried the fat man. "Well done! And you know what politicians do?"

"Yes," said Jeremy James. "They ruin the country."

"What?" said the fat man.

"They ruin the country," said Jeremy James again.

"Nonsense!" said the fat man. "Who's been telling you such nonsense?"

"Daddy," said Jeremy James.

Daddy turned a little red and shuffled his feet.

"Let me tell you," said the fat man, "this government is doing a splendid job, and everything in the garden is coming up roses."

"You mustn't tell fibs," said Jeremy James.

"I'm not telling fibs," said the fat man.

"Yes you are," said Jeremy James.

"No I'm not," said the fat man.

"Come along, dear," said the tall thin lady. "This is no time for a political discussion."

"There's always time for a political discussion," said the fat man. "Besides, the children of today are the voters of tomorrow."

"Well, you can worry about that tomorrow," said the tall thin lady.

The fat man frowned and looked straight at Daddy.

"You shouldn't tell your little boy such things," he said.

"Well if everything in the garden *was* coming up roses," said Daddy, "I wouldn't have to."

The fat man said something rather like "Hmmph!", and jelly-wobbled away.

"He does tell fibs, doesn't he Daddy?" asked Jeremy James.

"He certainly does," said Daddy.

"*And* he eats too many wrong things," said Jeremy James.

The Reverend Cole's legs heaved his body up the steps on to the platform, and the MP and his wife followed.

"Ah! Foof! Foof!" cried the Reverend Cole into the microphone. "Can you . . . ah . . . can you hear me?"

There were a few nods and cries of yes, including a loud one from Jeremy James.

"Let us begin with a short prayer," continued the Reverend Cole. "O almighty and most merciful God, of thy bountiful goodness keep us, we beseech thee, from all things that may hurt us . . ."

"Especially rain and politicians," murmured Daddy.

". . . that we, being ready both in body and soul, may cheerfully accomplish those things that Thou wouldst have done; through Jesus Christ our Lord."

There was a murmur of "Amen".

"What *is* 'Ah men'?" asked Jeremy James.

"The opposite of 'Ah women'," said Daddy.

"It means something like 'Let it be true'," said Mummy.

The Reverend Cole then welcomed everybody, and introduced the Right Honourable Cecil Ponsonby-Thistlethwaite MP, "just to say a few words".

"Amen," said Daddy.

"Lovely to see you all," said the fat man, "in spite of this dreadful weather. Please don't blame the government for that, ha ha!"

He waited for people to laugh, but nobody did. Then he went on to talk about himself and about the government, and about the government and about himself, and about how wonderful the government was, and about how wonderful he was, and... Jeremy James stopped listening and looked round the marquee.

There were quite a lot of people now, and they all seemed rather miserable. It was difficult to say if they were miserable because they were wet, or miserable because they were bored.

"I and the government will go on doing what's right and what's good..." said the fat man.

"This," murmured Daddy, "is a fête worse than death."

The wind screamed, and the rain drummed, but not even they could drown the endless drone of the fat man.

It was at this moment that Jeremy James happened to look up, and having looked up, he stayed looking up. What he saw reminded him very strongly of the fortune-teller. High above the head of the fat man, the roof of the marquee seemed to be bulging downwards, and there was a gap appearing between the roof and the side, as if an invisible hand was slowly pulling the two sections apart.

Jeremy James tugged Daddy's sleeve. Daddy looked down.

"Boring, eh?" whispered Daddy.

Jeremy James shook his head and pointed upwards. Daddy followed the direction of the point, and his eyes widened.

"Good Lord!" he said.

Jeremy James had not seen Daddy move so fast since Timothy had got stuck in the sea and Daddy had had to rush out and rescue him.

"Get off!" Daddy shouted, as he neared the platform. "Get off!"

". . . because the fact is, we know what's best for everyone . . ." the fat man was saying.

Daddy jumped up on to the platform, pointed upwards, and at once the Reverend Cole and the tall thin lady hurried down the steps.

"Cecil!" cried the lady.

". . . and you can put your trust in us—"

"Cecil!"

"Ssh! I'm talking, dear! And get that wretched man away from me! Damned Opposition agitators

everywhere. Believe me, ladies and gentlemen, we
know what we're doing, and your future is utterly
safe in our—"

But nobody heard what their future was utterly
safe in, because at that precise moment, the bulge in
the roof turned into an open flap, and down came
a great swooshing cataract of water. It had one
target only: the Right Honourable Cecil Ponsonby-
Thistlethwaite.

The drenching took only a couple of seconds, but
at the end of it, the fat man was standing on the
platform soaked through from head to toe, and dripping like a giant sponge.

At once some kind souls hurried to help him, and
he was led away gasping and spluttering.

"Thank you so much for saving me," the tall thin lady said to Daddy.

"It wasn't me," said Daddy. "It was Jeremy James who spotted it."

The lady came across to Jeremy James.

"I understand it was you who spotted the danger," she said.

"Yes," said Jeremy James.

"You're a very smart young man," said the lady, "and I want to thank you."

With that she reached into her purse, and pulled out a five pound note.

Jeremy James's eyes went as wide as the flap in the roof, and he gasped almost as loud as the fat man had done.

"Five pounds!" he cried. "Thank you very much!"

"When you grow up," said the lady, with the thinnest of thin smiles, "I think I might well be voting for you."

Then she hurried away to be with her husband.

Next it was the Reverend Cole who wanted to say thank you.

"Actually," he said to Daddy, "when you were shouting 'Get off!' I thought you were trying to stop him talking."

"It was a temptation," said Daddy. "But as things turned out, he stopped talking anyway, didn't he?"

"Ah!" said the Reverend Cole. "God moves in a mysterious way his wonders to perform."

Then the Reverend Cole thanked Jeremy James for spotting the danger, and put his hand in his pocket. Jeremy James began to go wide-eyed again, but instead of a five pound note, out came a handkerchief.

"Well done, Jeremy James," he said, wiping his nose. "You'll get your reward in Heaven."

The church fête really was ruined by the weather, and after the accident with the roof, most people wanted to leave the marquee as quickly as possible anyway. The guest of honour had wanted to leave it even more quickly than possible, and was not seen again that afternoon. But although the occasion had been such a disaster, everyone agreed that it had also been quite memorable. Certainly Mummy and Daddy were not the only people who were still laughing when they got home.

As for Jeremy James, he thought the fête had been a great success, and to prove it he had a five pound note and as many cakes as he could eat.

David Henry Wilson
Elephants Don't Sit on Cars

'Mummy,' said Jeremy James, 'there's an elephant sitting on Daddy's car and the car doesn't look very happy about it!'

'But elephants don't sit on cars,' said Mummy.

Or do they?

If there's trouble about – with elephants, babysitters, burglars, or a shopping trip to the supermarket – Jeremy James will find it.

David Henry Wilson
How to Stop a Train with One Finger

The train glided by, and he waved. He wished it would stop. But on it went . . . and on. They hadn't stopped at all!

Not everybody can stop a train with one finger, cause mad panic in the library and total destruction in the darkroom. But Jeremy James can . . . and does.

David Henry Wilson
Do Goldfish Go To Heaven?

'In that game of Freezing,' said Daddy, *'what exactly did you throw in the goldfish pond?'*

'The black box,' said Jeremy James.

'What black box?' asked Daddy.

'The one with Melissa's violin,' said Jeremy James.

Jeremy James is very good at solving problems like Melissa's violin, lost car keys and a missing Virgin Mary. But when it comes to paying bills, falling in the river, and turning yellow and purple, Jeremy James himself can be a bit of a problem . . .